Cliff House
&
Lands End

San Francisco's Seaside Retreat

by

Ariel Rubissow

Contents

The Golden Gate National Park Association is a non-profit membership organization established to support the education, conservation and research programs of the Golden Gate National Recreation Area.

PUBLISHED BY
GOLDEN GATE NATIONAL
PARK ASSOCIATION

ISBN 1-883869-12-9

Bone-chilling *winds,*

damp blank fogs, dark dangerous surf and turf — this is the stuff of San Francisco's seaside. Out around Lands End, you'll find a wild, rough corner of a tidy, gleaming city, an awesome boundary of a vast continent and even vaster ocean, and the headlands and beaches of the Golden Gate National Recreation Area.

And now and then, just when you're fed up with the raw conditions, the wind dies, the fog lifts and the sun blazes forth over an oceanfront as magnificent as any.

Indeed, it's just this kind of drama and contrast, this realm of colliding human and natural worlds, that has drawn people to San Francisco's Pacific coast since 500 A.D. Native Americans camped here to collect mussels and hunt seals. Early settlers rode over hill and dune to fish and gaze at the waves. Victorians flocked to the seaside to savor not only nature's offerings but also Sutro's. On the City's wild and windy ocean shore, millionaire Adolph Sutro built a fairy-like Cliff House, a formal statue garden and palatial swimming baths stocked with Egyptian mummies, stuffed anacondas and palm trees.

Although they've exchanged their long skirts and high hats for sweatshirts and sneakers, today's visitors to the San Francisco seaside make much the same pilgrimage as the Victorians. They follow the same scenic route along the clifftops from the Golden Gate to Ocean Beach, only this time via car and cycle rather than rail and buggy.

They enjoy the same thrilling views of ocean-carved headlands and Pacific horizons, only this time backed by skyscrapers and suspension bridges rather than shacks and Civil War forts.

They seek the same seaside sensations — the tingle of salt and sand spray on their cheeks, the roar and tumble of the ocean, the thrill of an infinite horizon, the solidity of earth and continent under their feet.

The Continent's Edge

IF YOU'D FANCIED A DAY at the seaside a hundred million years ago, a trip to the Cliff House would not have been your first choice. Back then, Lands End and San Francisco Bay lay lost in ocean floor oozes and the Pacific surf swept up to the Sierra.

If you'd chosen instead the Lands End of a mere twenty thousand years ago, you'd have found the seaside out beyond the Farallon Islands. You wouldn't have seen today's landscape of rocky cliffs and seashore until 7,000 years ago.

While people have added cypress forests, grand buildings and coast roads to the landscape, these changes barely scratch the surface compared to the colossal upheavals of geologic history. And people face a precarious future in a setting where ocean and continent continue to throw their weight around, and where earthquakes, landslides and erosive forces promise to tinker with the lay of the land for eons to come.

Birth of a Landscape

About 200 million years ago, the first building blocks of today's Golden Gate headlands began amassing thousands of miles away in the ocean deep. As the gigantic plates underlying the Pacific Ocean spread apart, molten lava poured out of cracks in a mid-ocean ridge and congealed into a new seafloor of basalt. Over the next 100 million years, the skeletons of microscopic marine organisms (radiolarians) settled through the water onto the basalt and slowly hardened from ooze into a rock called radiolarian chert.

The Farallon and Kula plates on the east side of the mid-oceanic ridge moved slowly (a few inches per year) toward North America, their leading edges sliding under the continent and leaving seafloor scrapings behind. But it wasn't until 29 million years ago that the mid-oceanic ridge encountered North America.

At this point, the eastbound Farallon plate largely disappeared under the westbound North American plate. This left the Pacific Plate on the other side of the ridge on a northwesterly tack parallel to the continent's edge. About 10 million years ago, the plate boundary jumped about a hundred miles east, giving birth to the San Andreas fault zone off Lands End today.

All this scraping, stacking and slipping between plates produced a hodge-podge of rocks geologists call the Franciscan Complex. The complex, now exposed at Lands End, includes the seafloor scrapings of basalt and chert, and sedimentary rocks such as sandstone and mudstone eroded from the continent's edge.

In the more recent stages of Lands End's geologic birth, about three million years ago, a slight change in direction of the Pacific Plate pushed up California's Coast Ranges. These new mountains cut off drainage from the Great (Central) Valley to the Pacific, forming a lake. The lake spilled over the lowest saddle in the Coast Ranges, around today's Carquinez Strait, and flowed out as a river between the Golden Gate headlands to the Pacific. The Golden Gate then became, as it is today, the only sea-level gap in the Coast Range.

In the last million years, ice ages lowered the sea level, exposing a plain of river-deposited sand between the Golden Gate and the Farallons. When the sea level rose again, waves and wind drove the sand eastward and mantled San Francisco and Lands End with dunes. With the addition of the weathered light-brown sands of this Colma Formation, the basic building blocks of San Francisco's headlands were in place.

Carving Out the Coast

Changes in the Lands End landscape continue to occur both on a monumental and minute scale. Imagine a rainy day in winter, for example, when water running off Point Lobos loosens a chunk of sandstone and sends it bouncing down the cliff. The sandstone chunk skips down a steep slope, sparking a minor landslide, and breaks into pieces upon impact with the shore. Waves toss and turn the pieces, wearing them down into grains small enough for a strong April seabreeze to blow inland into the dune grass where, over time, they combine with decaying stems and roots to form soil.

Whether solid rock or fine sand, the land mass at this continental edge has been at the daily mercy of erosive waves, tides and rain for millennia. These powerful natural forces constantly shape and reshape the Pacific coast. Take the beaches, for example. During the summer, Ocean Beach can be up to a hundred feet wider than in the winter. Winter's steep, stormy waves carry more sand seaward, lowering the beach by up to six feet. Summer's broad, flat waves drive the sand back shoreward, restoring the beach to its former level.

The pounding waves of the Pacific, which occasionally roll in all the way from Japan, not only shape beaches but also coastal cliffs. On a local scale, the waves remove blocks and grains of rock, steepening and undermining cliffs. The constant wetting and drying also swells, shrinks and fragments the rock.

Typical rocks of the Franciscan Complex: greenstone with quartz intrusions (top); greywacke (middle); and radiolarian chert (reddish) surrounded by greenstone (bottom).

On a larger scale, waves shape whole headlands. Where the headlands jut out, the underlying rock is harder and more resistent; where they dip inland around coves, the rock may be softer.

Many soft spots contain easily eroded Franciscan melange, a paste of crushed rock and water-absorbing clay. Wet clay buoys up surrounding rock, and smoothes the way for landslides. Ongoing slumps and slides at Lands End have wiped out railroads and trails, shifted whole hillsides to the base of the cliffs, and left behind many a death-dealing foothold for careless passersby.

Though landslides wreak havoc on the headlands, they also protect them from further erosion by depositing big boulders along the shore. This natural riprap helps deflect waves.

Colonizing the Cliffs and Sands

Many of the native plants that colonized Lands End have leaves, roots and stems specially adapted to the volatile nature of the terrain. The farther back from the ocean's edge, the more soil and water are available to sustain them. However, almost every flora species on this exposed edge of the continent has to contend with harsher conditions than those inland.

The dunes closest to shore offer scarce moisture, high winds and shifting sand. Yet many beautiful, colorful plants find ways to grow here, including yellow-flowered sand verbena, beach primrose and coastal strawberry. All of these species share certain characteristics key to their survival — thick leaves to hold water, low growth to stay out of the wind, and extensive root systems enabling them to survive recurring burial under sand drifts.

Sand verbena

Farther inland, plant species don't have to be quite so flexible. Here in the rear dunes, the small amount of accumulating organic matter gradually develops just enough soil and water to support taller, woodier and more deeply rooted flora such as mock heather, coastal sage and dune tansy.

The gentle coastal bluffs beyond the dunes offer still more soil and water, sustaining coyote brush, monkeyflower and bush lupine. Higher up on the clifftops, shallow-rooted purple needlegrass and California oat grass spread inland.

Add this final element of vegetation to the earth-shaping geologic and erosive processes of nature and you have the landscape that greeted the first people to visit this wave-lashed edge of the continent.

Early Life on the Oceanfront

The Ohlone Indians first came to Lands End from inland villages in search of food. They pried mussels, clams and whelks from rocky terraces exposed by low tide; they caught ducks with handwoven seine nets; they clubbed seals and sea lions hauled out on the sands below. They searched the nooks and crannies of the cliffs for seabird eggs, stalked deer across the grassy bluffs, and trapped otters prized for their supple, waterproof skin. Now and then a whale would strand on the beach, providing meat and blubber butter for months on end.

Mounds of refuse, called middens, mark these early Native American sites. Archaeologists first discovered three middens at Lands End in 1901. Since no building materials or utensils turned up in the middens, excavators concluded that the Native Americans gathered here to hunt and process food before packing it back to their homes on the more hospitable leeward side of the San Francisco peninsula. Fire-cracked rocks and a large hearth emerged from the rubble around today's Sutro Baths area, conjuring up an historic picture of Native American activities on the headlands.

In that thousand-year-old picture, a small cove filled what would later become the site of the Sutro Baths. On the bluffs above, a ring of fires burned where Ohlones cooked fish and meat, and dried skins. Some sat on the edge of the cliff looking out over the ocean, shucking mussels and tossing the shells at their feet. Some butchered and skinned sea lions on the beach, removing bones and other parts too heavy to transport back to their villages. Some fanned out over the surrounding cliffs and shores to harvest the abundant food available from both land and sea.

Studies of the middens indicate that the Ohlones probably used these sites from around 500 A.D. until the first Spanish explorers arrived in 1769. The development of the Spanish and Mexican missions brought an end to the Ohlone way of life, as well as changes to the ecology and use of the peninsula's headlands. The Spanish introduced hoof-resistent Mediterranean grasses to the bluffs, and grazed their livestock in the area.

By the early 1800s, Lands End lay within a large Mexican land grant named Rancho Punta de Lobos after the sea "wolves" whose cries filled the air.

Though few of the first European settlers chose to live on the inhospitable ocean side of the peninsula, some visited the beach and headlands for the same reasons as the Ohlones. According to one early report, fish were so plentiful fishermen could just grab them straight out of the surf with their bare hands.

VERY LITTLE IS LEFT OF Lands End's Indian middens today, thanks to the 19th- and 20th-century building activity of Adolph Sutro and the U.S. Army. But over the years, the subsequent occupants of San Francisco's headlands continued the ocean-gazing and cooking activities begun by the Native Americans, only this time in the settings of parks and restaurants.

"The waves arriving here daily at the city's doorstep are the visible symbols of the basic rhythms of the earth—the rolling waters, the rising tides, the cyclonic storms and rivers of air that flow across the face of the planet." Harold Gilliam, *Natural World of San Francisco*

Two small groves provided all the genetic material for the millions of cypress that have since been planted worldwide.

Windy Woods

A natural world of dark forests surrounds the well-known recreational landmarks of Lands End today. These Monterey cypress and pine did not appear naturally on the bare coastal bluffs, however. They were planted by the City, the Army and local landowners.

While not native to San Francisco, these trees come from nearby Monterey.

The 60- to 80-foot-tall cypress is tenacious enough to grow in the harsh conditions at the continent's edge. "Battered by wind and stung by salt spray," writes journalist Harold Gilliam, "the cypresses grip the [rock] with gnarled roots, build buttresses to the leeward, and lean away from the onslaught of the ocean and weather. . . [which sculpt] them into fantastic, contorted forms that seem lineal continuations of the ancient wave-worn rocks."

Fierce Pacific winds prune these evergreens — breaking off frail branches and leaving behind stronger limbs sandwiched between breezeways. Trees closest to the ocean often act as windfoils, directing winds via their wedged shapes up and over inner trees.

Just inland from the edge of the cliffs, in elegant gray forests clear of underbrush, grow the taller and more stately Monterey pines. This long-needled conifer can grow over two feet a year for decades on end.

Unlike their cousins in the primeval groves of the Pacific Northwest, these forests experience extreme impacts both from nature and the metropolis next door. Human feet trample their roots, and erosive forces remove soil and outer windfoil trees. Meanwhile, the close spacing of the original planting leaves little room for new growth and fire remains absent from the natural forest regeneration process.

S

Sunday by the Sea

WHEN PROVIDENCE SPRINKLED gold dust on San Francisco in the 1850s, it transformed a frontier outpost into a lively metropolis. Hotels, bars and businesses sprang up on every available inch of space, but the new development stopped short when it encountered the sand dune wilderness. Locals named this inaccessible zone the Outside Lands.

Despite the difficult six-mile journey across the dunes to the City's western shore — a ride guaranteed to leave the traveler saddlesore and sandburned — there were always a few adventurous souls who couldn't resist the call of the Pacific on a Sunday afternoon. Some liked to stroll or ride along the beach; some delighted in the fat seals and sea lions lounging on the offshore rocks and playing in the surf; some gorged on the patch of wild strawberries covering one bluff. But more than anything, these visitors sought the company of the ocean.

As one writer explained in an 1859 issue of *California Magazine*: "There is a never ceasing pleasure to a refined mind, in looking upon or listening to the hoarse murmuring roar of the sea; and an unexplainable charm in the music of its waves, as with a seething sound, they curl and gently break upon a sandy shore, during a calm; or dash in all their majesty and fury, with thundering voices on the unheeding rocks in a storm. This is sublimity."

Early Settlers and Visitors

Only one settler — a man named Chambers — dared to live on the far edge of the Outside Lands. Chambers homesteaded 160 acres of the bluffs in the mid-1800s, and planted potatoes. Though locals regarded his crop as the finest on the peninsula, he had trouble transporting it across the sands to market. By the time real estate tycoon Charles Butler wandered out to the shoreline in 1854, Chambers had moved to a more advantageous location in Oregon.

Butler explored the beach and bluffs on horseback, sampled the wild strawberries, and considered the development potential of the area. He envisioned a row of fine oceanfront mansions with wraparound verandas inhabited by the very best of families — including his own. And in the back of his mind Butler remembered his father urging him to look out for the piece of land that would become the San Francisco equivalent of New York's Coney Island. Perhaps, he thought, as he admired the City's Pacific shore, this was it.

While Butler explored and dreamed, others built the shoreline's first two saloons — Ocean House and Seal Rock House. Hauling timber to this far-flung corner of the City wasn't cheap, and stories of the origins of both these new establishments trace the source of their building materials to shipwrecks on the beach.

Early excursionists soon made the two saloons part of a scenic loop. They set off from Fort Point, travelled along the clifftop trail to Seal Rock House at the north end of Ocean Beach, stopped for a hot toddy, continued south down the hard shore sands, and ducked into Ocean House at the south end of the beach for additional refreshment in preparation for the return trip home via the old mission trail. This was no easy excursion, but for hardy ocean lovers it soon became a favorite Sunday outing.

Grand Schemes for the San Francisco Seaside

The more Butler thought about it, the more he realized the row of elegant oceanfront mansions wasn't enough. He soon expanded his plans for the strawberry patch and the surrounding 160 acres to include a fashionable seaside resort — a step in the direction of his father's Coney Island.

First, he cast around for a way to make the area more accessible to the big-spenders in San Francisco. By the early 1860s, Butler had formed the Point Lobos Road Company with State Senator John Buckley, and work began. Butler sent one team of laborers to grade and fill the sand dunes at the end of Bush Street and another to carve a route out of what the newspapers dubbed "the oceanbound precipitous steeps" at Point Lobos.

As work on the 110-foot-wide, macadamized (broken stone bound by mineral pitch) toll road progressed, Butler supervised construction of its terminus — the first Cliff House. He sited this simple, one-story frame-and-clapboard structure on a ledge so close to the water that, as one reporter put it, patrons could "pitch a biscuit into the sea" from their seats.

Butler installed Captain Junius Foster at the helm of his new resort. Foster made sure the Cliff House offered just what the wealthy Victorians desired — a plush parlor with fabulous ocean views "where but a single pane of glass seemed to separate the comforts and refinements of civilization and peace from the rude jarring of elemental discord and Nature in her rudest aspect, beyond," according to local author Bret Harte.

High society took to the place immediately. Everyone dining there knew everybody. And in those days *everybody* meant the Stanfords, Crockers, Hearsts, Vandewaters, Lathams and other prominent families whose names still crown the mastheads of San Francisco's banks, universities and newspapers. One disapproving (and poor) journalist wrote: "The Cliff House is a fashionable resort visited by fashionable people, who dance and flirt, walk or ride on the beach and indulge in all the dissipation it is possible for persons to engage in."

Business went so well at the Cliff House that Foster tripled its size in 1868, adding two new wings. On the sheltered inland side he built a big sunning platform; on the seaward side, a broad veranda adaptable to dancing.

With the Cliff House at the other end, Butler's new Point Lobos toll road flourished. An 1871 tourist guide described it as the "broadest, hardest, smoothest and longest track in the state. A million dollars' worth of legs and wheels flash by a man in a very few hours on this fashionable drive." Butler made a one-and-a-half-mile section of the track into a clay speedway, which was frequently rolled and watered so that the owners of fast trotters pulling phaetons, hacks, landaus and barouches could race their way to the Cliff House.

"A drive to the 'Cliff' in the early morning, a hearty welcome from Captain Foster, and an hour passed over his hospitable board discussing the choice contents of his larder, and a return to the city through the charming scenery of Golden Gate Park, tends to place man about as near to elysian bliss as he may hope for in this world." B.E. Lloyd, 1876

Beach Amusements

Mooneysville and the penny gaffs launched a string of oceanfront amusements that lasted until 1960. In the 1890s, Adolph Sutro installed a ferris wheel, maze and haunted spring just up the road from the Cliff House. Down on the sandy flats several decades later, Playland at the Beach attracted weekend mobs in the tens of thousands, all clamoring to ride the Big Dipper roller coaster, explore the Maze of Mirrors, or get soaked while shooting the Chutes. Afterwards, visitors indulged in an Its-Its ice cream cookie bar. Between 1929 and 1960, a visit to Playland and the adjacent beach was one of the most popular San Francisco outings.

At the same time, the City completed a new road to the Ocean House further south. The two roads, connected by a wheel-worthy stretch of beach, replaced the sandy trail loop of the past. On weekends, a steady stream of sightseers made the circuit to admire the ocean panoramas, see the sea lions, or dash their carriages through the surf. By March 1863, the Sunday crowd at the beach had swelled to a thousand. By 1870, as many as 1,200 teams tied up at the Cliff House on a weekend day.

New Visitors and Patrons

The Cliff House remained exclusive since the high prices on its menu, and the costs of owning a horse and rig and paying the road tolls to get there, kept ordinary folk away. Over the years, however, improved transportation made the area more accessible to the general public — much to the chagrin of the high-society Cliff House clientele. They didn't like to mix, so they stayed away.

When Captain Foster began losing business, he opened his doors to a faster set of San Franciscans. To better accommodate this gold-rich sporting society of gamblers, hookers and Barbary Coast lowlifes, Foster hired pretty young women as barmaids, ordered more card tables, and outfitted the private parlors upstairs with satin sofas and ornate door bolts. In exchange, his new and naughty patrons paid handsomely for the privilege of partying in a manner one newspaper described as "orgiastic."

These new clients, in turn, frowned on the arrival of out-of-town tourists and so, on occasion, did their proprietor. Foster liked to tell of the 340 visitors from Massachusetts who spent all day at the Cliff House and ordered nothing but three lemonades (and 200 glasses of water).

Recreation on the Waterfront

In many ways, Butler's long-ago visit to Strawberry Hill not only inspired the first vision of a western Coney Island but also launched a pilgrimage to the Pacific shore that was to become a San Francisco tradition. In the decades that Butler owned the 160-acre former potato and strawberry patch, the City's western shore evolved from a rugged, wave-lashed wilderness to a major recreational development where locals savored both the beach and the entertainment presented for their amusement.

On a rainy, windy day in 1865, Foster invited the public to see Captain James Cooke walk a tightrope strung 70 feet above the roiling surf between south Seal Rock and the Cliff House. Despite the bad weather, 15,000 onlookers gathered and cheered wildly when Captain Cooke emerged in pink tights at the far end of the rope. Cooke stuck one foot out on the rope and gave up, pitching his balancing pole into the sea. But he returned again the next week and succeeded in completing the feat.

When Leonardo da Vinci invented the camera obscura in the 16th century, his neighbors regarded it as an instrument of the devil. But since then, it has aided Copernicus with charting the stars, Renaissance artists with painting, and Cliff House visitors with scanning the scenery. The giant walk-in camera, first erected on the San Francisco shore in the early 1900s, offers those who look through its periscope a rotating view of the cliffs, rocks, waves and walls outside. Ansel Adams indulged in this parabolic view so often that they gave up charging the budding young photographer an entrance fee.

In the 1870s and '80s, crowds enjoyed other similar spectacles including "Millie's" slide along a wire by her teeth to Seal Rocks, and Thomas Baldwin's jump from a balloon poised a thousand feet over the beach. During his jump, Baldwin dangled from a new-fangled invention called a parachute.

When the City laid a railroad line to the beach in the early 1880s, a little shanty town of quick-dollar vendors sprang up around the terminus. The newspapers called the town Mooneysville after Don Mooney — a squatter who hired fiddlers and set them up on a beach-front dance floor in 1883. Though Mooneysville didn't survive long, other merchants soon launched beach ventures ranging from a pretentious pavilion to seaside shacks proffering peanuts and penny gaffs.

THE "CLIFF" CONTINUED to hold sway in the 1870s by having "the view, the seals, the music, the host, and the stamp of fashion," according to the *Daily Alta Californian*, but it entered the 1880s somewhat tarnished by the scandalous goings-on inside. By this time, however, the area's future as a recreational hotspot was firmly dug into the dunes. And Butler would live to see his resort move a giant step closer to Coney Island proportions through the efforts of another man — Adolph Sutro.

Seal Rocks

Seal Rocks are now a bird kingdom rarely disturbed by the barks of sea lions. Here, Brandts cormorants and western gulls nest among the rocks out of reach of predators. In the fall, brown pelicans stop off for a snooze between fishing trips.

Not so long ago, California and Steller sea lions used the rocks as an important haul-out spot but swam to more remote locations to bear and raise their pups. Both species suffered from commercial hunting in the 1800s, when hunters sold their whiskers for pipe cleaners, their hides for purses, and their genitals for aphrodisiacs. In the 1880s, local fishermen blamed sea lions for their poor catch, and lobbied to place a bounty on their heads. Fortunately, Adolph Sutro, who often spent hours watching the sea lions from his clifftop home, convinced Congress to make Seal Rocks the nation's first marine sanctuary.

One sea lion earned recognition for being the largest of his day. Named Ben Butler after a droopeyed, mustachioed politician and Civil War general, the sea lion became such a local celebrity that when he died Sutro had him stuffed so he could preside over the rocks from a Sutro Baths exhibit in perpetuity.

In recent decades, West Coast sea lion populations have diminished

The two species differ in size and color, with Steller sea lions larger (1,500-2,000 pounds a piece) and lighter, and the darker California sea lions weighing in at a mere 600-800 pounds.

due to poor food supplies, pollution, human disturbance and other factors. In 1991, the federal government declared the Steller sea lion a threatened species. In 1990, counts placed California population figures at only 10 percent of 1930s levels. In the same time period, the Seal Rock colony dipped from a few hundred to a handful.

Though Steller sea lions are the larger and more aggressive species (they even eat California sea lion pups), biologists have found them finicky eaters that are highly susceptible to human disturbance. It is the more opportunistic California sea lions, which will seemingly eat anything that swims their way, that have made the most of current San Francisco conditions. Abandoning suburban Seal Rocks in the early 1990s, they moved into the City claiming some of Pier 39's docks for their own.

"...if there be in the whole animal kingdom any creature of size and sound less adapted than a sea [lion] as a public pet, I do not know such creature's name... Shapeless, boneless, limbless, and featureless, neither fish nor flesh; of the color and consistency of India-rubber...; slipping, clinging, sticking, like gigantic leeches; flapping, wallowing with unapproachable clumsiness; lying still, lazy, inert, asleep, apparently, till they are baked browner and hotter than they like, then plunging off the rocks, turning once over in the water to wet themselves enough to bear more baking; and all the while making a noise too hideous to be described — a mixture of bray and squeal and snuff and snort..."   Helen Hunt Jackson

The shape of each rock inspired Adolph Sutro to give them individual names: Repose Rock, Lone Rock, Arch Rock and Hermit Rock.

For those who enjoyed flying through air before swimming through water, Sutro Baths offered nine springboards, seven toboggan slides, three trapezes, thirty swinging rings, and several high diving platforms. For spectators, Sutro trotted out numerous airborne entertainers including Jack, the highest diving dog in the world, and Charmian, girl aerialist and Queen of the Air.

"Many a San Franciscan remembers his first childhood sight of the fairyland-like baths. Once through the ticket gate, with rented towel, suit and locker key clasped firmly in hand, he stood upon a balcony that seemed to float like a cloud above the shimmering pools far below. All around him was the echoing, enveloping sound of splash and laughter and shouts; the close feel of heat and high humidity; the engrossing smell compounded of salt water dampness, wet cloth, human bodies and frying hotdogs."

John F. Allen
San Francisco Examiner

August 28, 1952

Whoever places
a seed in
the earth
is king over
unreckoned
forces

𝑆

Sutro's Folly

ON A FOGGY DAY IN 1850, twenty-year-old Prussian-born engineer Adolph Sutro sailed through the Golden Gate on the steamer *California*. He couldn't see much of the headlands where he was later to build one of the City's first parks, one of the world's largest swimming pools, and one of the state's most popular recreational complexes by the sea. What he thought about that day, as he searched the mists for the young City, was his prospects for making a fortune in a gold-rich state and a promised land.

He began with two bales of German cloth and two trunks of fancy European notions and soon owned several tobacco shops in downtown San Francisco. But it was in the muddy, dirty mining towns of "Washoe Country," Nevada that he made his real fortune and earned his nickname — the Comstock King.

At that time, the miners of the Comstock lode — a multi-million dollar vein of gold and silver — battled with hellish conditions. "The miners, in hot water up to their necks, worked in shifts of fifteen minutes, then dashed to inhale at nozzles air blown down to them by great fans," wrote one historian of the day. "They worked in steam that reeked like rotten eggs."

Sutro designed and built a tunnel to drain and ventilate the mines. It took him 15 years of battling with bank monopolies, mine owners, investors and senators. But once the four-mile tunnel pierced the lode and proved its worth, everyone congratulated Sutro for accomplishing the greatest engineering feat of the era.

At the age of 49, his coal black hair and handlebar moustache gone white, the Comstock King sold his tunnel stock and returned to San Francisco a millionaire.

Cottage for a King

Sutro's boyhood botany teacher said something that Sutro remembered all his life: "Live ever near to nature's heart, for to depart from nature is a departure from happiness." On a March day in 1881, Sutro embraced this philosophy when he pressed a $1,000 down payment into Sam Tetlow's hands for the music hall owner's home by the

Sutro collected art and literature from all over the world, and planned to build a fine public library. He owned a first folio of Shakespeare, Father Junipero Serra's Bible, and volumes once treasured by England's dukes and duchesses. His collection of 250,000 volumes included a book printed in every year between 1464 and 1885. Until the 1906 earthquake and fire destroyed a third of this collection, he owned the nation's largest private library. Part of the surviving collection can be found at San Francisco's Sutro Library.

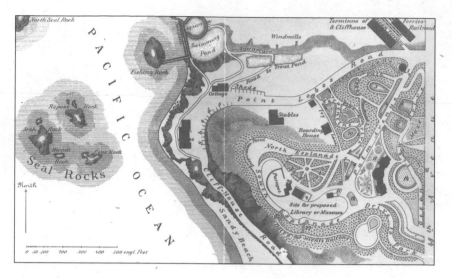

Plan of Sutro Heights,
Cliff House & Seal Rocks

sea. Tetlow's cottage perched on a rocky promontory overlooking ocean, beach, headlands and sea lions. There was little vegetation except for a few strawberries dating back to the time when Tetlow's acreage encompassed Butler's Strawberry Hill and Chamber's potato patch.

Although Sutro went on to purchase most of San Francisco's Outside Lands and other real estate adding up to a fifth of the City's total area, the cottage and surrounding acreage became the nucleus and inspiration point for the "folly" that was to engage Sutro for the rest of his life — turning the rugged dunes, rocks and coastline into gardens and resorts accessible to all San Franciscans.

Rather than tearing down Tetlow's cottage and erecting a millionaire's mansion, Sutro made modest renovations and added an observation tower and glass-enclosed porch. True to his teacher's philosophy, he spent more money on the grounds outside his front door than on the interior of his home.

A Garden on the Heights

Sutro set out not only to maximize the extraordinary ocean vistas from the cottage grounds but also to create a sheltered environment for the many beautiful flowers and trees he hoped to grow. He ordered species tolerant of drought and seaside conditions from as far away as the Black Sea coast and North Africa; hired gardeners and laborers to prepare the site; installed a watering system powered by windmills; laid out paths and promenades; and constructed a parapet wall overlooking the sea complete with 30 stone crenellations reminiscent of an English castle.

He also planted windbreaks of eucalyptus, cypress and pine; built a glass conservatory for sensitive tropical plants; and arranged for 200 statues of historic personages and mythological deities to be sent from Belgium. It cost twice as much to convey the sculptures across the six miles of dunes between the wharf and the Heights as it did to ship them across the Atlantic and around Cape Horn to San Francisco.

APART FROM THE PARAPET, the new garden at the Heights had several special features. Looking south, a hanging balcony offered a romantic spot for lovers to enjoy the view. Sutro named the balcony *Dolce Far Niente* or "sweet to do nothing" in Italian. He planted a cluster of trees called the Old Grove as a shady canopy over a lawn. Eight axial walkways radiated from the grove and — in combination with floral tapestries and sculpted hedges — gave Sutro Heights the look of a formal garden. As a reporter from the *Pacific Rural Press* noted in 1886, the resulting garden "would put to the blush many a site where the owner had naturally rich soil and natural shelter for his allies."

Sutro opened his private garden to the public, inviting the urban populace to enjoy the vistas, open spaces and European sculpture. In an 1880s newspaper article on Sutro Heights, the writer passed between the two elegant lions at the main gate and found himself transported "from desert to paradise... Settees were invitingly placed to tempt one to rest and behold its grandeur... I watched a living fawn grazing the succulent grass... saw a reclining statue of a large buck..." Sutro's statues crowned the parapet crenellations, hid in the forest recesses, played in the mosses, presided over carriageways. There were characters from Charles Dickens, Greek gods such as Mercury and Apollo, and cats chasing mice on the green. Every year, these plaster sculptures received a fresh coat of white paint.

Another visitor wrote "The wilderness of sand has bloomed and blossomed into a scene of fairylike beauty. The air is redolent with fragrant shrubs and flowers, peace and calm and sunshine seem to reign perennially... Winding walks, fringed with beds of exquisite flowers, show bright and sunny against the green of trees of every shade from the darkest to the lightest... Lawns whose tender and delicate green can compare with that of England, broad carriage drives and esplanades from which the ever-changing face of the ocean is visible, all testify to the soundness of imagination that could devise and the practical skill that put into execution this work of beauty."

The tansy was just one of many delicate native flowers displaced by bigger, brighter exotics during Sutro's planting bonanza on the oceanfront.

"As one stands upon the esplanade which Mr. Sutro has carved from the native rock and set about with statues from the home of art beside the Mediterranean," still another visitor concluded, "one can but harbor the thought that intellectually, as well as otherwise, the course of empire has really taken its way westward until the placid waters of the Pacific declare its journey done."

In a city where the nearest thing to a park was the local cemetery, and where Golden Gate Park was still struggling to take root in the dunes, Sutro Heights became the most popular recreational destination in town. It took 11 gardeners and thousands of dollars to keep the 20-acre park groomed and blooming, but Sutro's folly didn't stop at the garden gate.

From Hanky Panky to Sugar Candy

Sutro bought the Cliff House and several miles of adjacent shoreline in 1881. But things didn't really change much until he hired James Wilkins to transform the ill-reputed establishment into a "respectable resort with no bolts on the doors or beds in the house." The bolts came off, the prices went down, the gamblers retreated, and families began frequenting the place. Sutro added collections of shells and rare coins.

On January 15, 1887, the two-masted schooner *Parallel* wrecked on the Cliff House rocks. The crew abandoned ship, leaving the schooner to the pounding Pacific. At midnight, the wave action set off the 42 tons of black powder in the *Parallel*'s hold. The explosion woke the entire City and damaged the Cliff House — smashing windows, lifting doors off hinges, and tearing down sheets of plaster. The *San Francisco Chronicle* speculated that had the explosion been a trifle more severe, the Cliff House would have fallen off the cliff into the sea.

Sutro and Wilkins repaired the Cliff House, only to see it go up in flames on Christmas Day in 1894. One onlooker examined the building's remains — a carved lion, two chimneys and a heap of ash — and called for Sutro to rebuild. "We don't want anything Romanesque or Arabesque. No Greek temple, Egyptian shrine or Queen Anne Freaks. [Just] a plain, old fashioned Cliff House like that was burned up," he said.

Clifftop Botanist

Sutro brought flowers and forests to the barren hills and coast of San Francisco. In 1886, he launched the first California Arbor Day with poet Joaquin Miller, during which 30,000 school children planted his cypress and eucalyptus seedlings in parks and their own backyards. On the same day, Sutro's own gardeners added millions more, laying out the wooded crowns of Sutro Heights, the Presidio, Fort Mason and Yerba Buena Island. By 1886, California recognized Sutro as one of its leading authorities on arbor culture. Sutro regarded his trees as the children of his old age. "Whoever places a seed in the earth is king over unreckoned forces," he said.

Railroad Wars

Sutro made sure that the public could get to his resort without going broke by developing his own rail line. When he sold the line's franchise to another company in 1887, he forced them to maintain an affordable five-cent fare. The new Ferries and Cliff House Railroad, with its open air cars, skirted the Lands End cliffs. One rider wrote "you might get a few shivers when you looked down... you were hanging right on the brink." In 1893, a Southern Pacific subsidiary took over the line and increased the fare to ten cents. Sutro appealed to the new owners to reinstate the old fare, and when they refused, he declared war. He fenced his properties, charged an entrance fee to all railroad riders (rail ticket sales soon dropped by 75 percent), began building a competing line, and encouraged Congress to break the stranglehold of the "Octopus" (Southern Pacific) on the American people. Largely as a result of Sutro's lobbying, Congress rejected a bill that would have delayed payment of the railroad's debt to the federal government. Not long afterwards, Southern Pacific dropped their fare.

218.   Bathing Beach, Cliff House, San Francisco, Cal.

Seaside recreation still revolves around the Cliff House—centerpiece of San Francisco's shore for over 130 years—as surely as it did in the humble days of its first incarnation and and during the grand times of its Victorian opulence.

Unfortunately, the onlooker had little pull with the Comstock King, for what Sutro eventually constructed was "an enormous chateau-like confection which many regarded as a monstrosity," according to the press. The confection was designed by architects Emile Lemme and C.J. Colley, whom Sutro had instructed to create a resort like San Diego's Hotel del Coronado.

The new five-story Cliff House rose 200 feet above the ocean and overhung the cliff — anchored by giant iron rods to the rocks. There was a magnificent central tower and four corner turrets, all topped with spires and decorated with carved white wood. Guests at the formal opening in February, 1896, found tourist concessions on the first floor, restaurants and dining rooms on the second, twenty private lunch rooms and an art gallery on the third, and more galleries, parlors and a 16-foot-wide oceanside veranda on the fourth floor. They made themselves comfortable in the many settees and easy chairs Sutro had provided for contemplation of the sea. And they feasted on a lavish opening banquet over which Sutro presided "like a contented Caesar," according to the *San Francisco Morning Call.*

Despite the disapproving clucks of the City's self-appointed style critics, the public loved Sutro's gingerbread palace. Throughout the 1890s, the resort enjoyed a second wave of popularity and served drinks and fine food to James Flood, Claus Spreckels, Mark Twain, Bret Harte, Sarah Bernhardt, Presidents McKinley, Roosevelt and Taft, and thousands of lesser-known locals.

« 33 »

Warm Baths by a Cold Ocean

Sutro's folly found perhaps its most fanciful expression in what someone called the "strange, sprawling, rococo, crystal palace" of

Sutro Baths. The project had its origins in the aquarium Sutro ingeniously constructed using the natural features of a small cove north of the Cliff House. The aquarium consisted of a rocky basin stocked with local sea life at high tide, and exposed by low tide.

Always the engineer, Sutro expanded this concept of using the natural cycles of

In 1898, Sutro Baths had 1,965 ladies bathing suits, 13,491 mens suits, and 5,000 towels for rent. Swimmers weren't allowed to bring their own attire due to sanitary standards, and the bath house laundries were equipped to sanitize up to 20,000 suits a day.

the ocean to supply his bath water — that is, the 1,685,000 gallons needed to fill the six pools of the three-acre glass bathhouse he had in mind.

Controlling nature enough to build a bath house at the edge of a wave-swept, crumbling continent proved difficult. It took two years and three attempts to erect the enormous 400 foot-long, 25- to 75-foot-wide breakwater to protect this new bath house from the Pacific. Boulders slated for the breakwater kept sinking into the sand, workmen kept falling into the surf, and foundations kept eroding away.

A million dollars and thousands of barrels of concrete later, Sutro opened his fabulous baths to the public. Bathers entered through a Greek temple, descended a wide stairway lined with palms, then either drifted over to the museum gallery to examine stuffed animals, curios and artifacts from the four corners of the world, or ducked into the changing rooms to pull on a wooly swimsuit. For their recreation and exercise, Sutro provided six saltwater swimming tanks of various shapes, sizes and water temperatures, one freshwater plunge tank and numerous diving boards and swings. Adjacent to the baths rose tier upon tier of bleachers. Overhead arched a roof sporting 100,000 square feet of stained glass and affording direct views of the ocean and sky.

When they opened, one contemporary writer stated that the baths rivaled "in magnitude, utility and beauty the famous ablution resorts of Titus, Caracalla, Nero or Diocletion."

While the critics extolled Sutro's engineering ingenuity and architectural skill, the public rejoiced. At last, there was water warm enough for swimming in San Francisco. Thousands of people jammed the baths on weekends.

Sutro's Legacy

Only a few years after he'd completed his seaside wonderland — expressing the extraordinary breadth of his scientific and artistic interests in the buildings and gardens — Adolph Sutro died. He was 68. His biographers, Robert and Mary Frances Stewart, wrote that he would have liked his funeral day. "The fog shrouded gardens of Sutro Heights were his temple and the plaintive barking of the [seals] his funeral dirge."

After his death, Sutro's daughter, Dr. Emma Merritt, struggled to maintain her father's legacy. When the grandiose Cliff House burned down in 1907, she put off rebuilding. It was indeed a sad moment. Historian Albert Tolf reflected that Sutro's Cliff House "closed with one catastrophic blaze ... as if to symbolize the end of an age of Victorian splendor ... of spacious times which couldn't have been crowded into the hurried age that followed."

Eventually, however, that hurried age ushered in a third neo-classical Cliff House designed by Reid Brothers — architects of San Francisco's famed Fairmont Hotel. This third Cliff House, though much renovated and modified, still offers an oceanfront watering hole and eatery today.

The Cliff House's splendid glass neighbor, Sutro Baths, flourished until 1937, when the Comstock King's grandson Gustav Sutro converted part of the baths into an ice rink. By 1966, a developer planned to raze the historic bathhouse to make way for a 200-unit

Baths Bricabrac
Sutro jammed the balconies of Sutro Baths with interesting artifacts. There were Aztec pots and Chinese swords, a piece of lava and 19 fans, a bird egg collection and an Indian skull, even the stump of a palm tree under which the fabled English explorer Captain Cook was killed. Stuffed animals looked back at visitors with glassy eyes: 60 parrots, a polar bear, a giant anaconda snake wrapped around a ferocious jaguar. Perhaps most curious was Mr. Ito, a lifesized lifelike self-portrait by a Japanese artist complete with hairs plucked from his own body. Sutro referred to these treasures as "bricabrac that will ... help install in the minds of youthful visitors a desire for learning."

apartment and restaurant complex by the sea. Public sentiment went against him, however, when a fire burned the City's beloved crystal palace to the foundations — leaving the strange, sand-swept ruin visible today.

Of all Sutro's accomplishments, the one he most loved and cared for remains the one best preserved today — Sutro Heights. Although Sutro's home, conservatory and fancy flower beds are long gone, and although vandals long ago shattered most of the original statues, the lawns, trees, parapet and rock gardens of the park remain intact — not to mention the unparalleled views of the coast.

In the 1970s, the National Park Service acquired the Sutro properties. They carefully stowed the few remaining statues in their museum collection and reproduced and reinstated others — including the entrance lions and the goddess Diana, who can often be found with a garland of leaves or other offering around her neck or at her feet.

Modest renovations have kept the Cliff House open. And visitors can explore the ruins of the baths while keeping an eye out for sneaker waves — freak waves that "sneak" up on visitors and sweep them away.

THROUGH THE PARK SERVICE, Sutro's commitment to public recreation on the San Francisco seaside remains alive and well almost a century after his death. This great man's last wishes are well-documented and embody his lifelong desire to be close to nature and the love he felt for the fruits of his folly. "Bury me where I can watch the ocean and rocks, bury me at Sutro Heights," he said.

"It is man's labor, and the heroic deeds of men, which put a new and more divine seal to nature's finest scenes."
—Adolph Sutro

Wrecks on the Rocks

In the days before fog horns came to the California coast, ship captains listened for the loud barks of the seal lions on Seal Rocks to guide them between the treacherous headlands of the Golden Gate channel. Despite these and later navigational aids, many a ship wrecked on the rocks off Lands End. In one spot, two barnacle-encrusted engine blocks and a rusty rudder post stick out of the water — last remains of the Frank Buck *and* Lyman Stewart. *These two tankers, built side-by-side in the same San Francisco shipyard, also ended their days on the same rocks in the early 1900s.*

Nearby Ocean Beach, where the surf swirls danger-ously around a sand bar, was the scene of 50 maritime accidents between 1850 and 1936, among them the clip-per King Philip *whose worn ribs can still be seen on the winter beach. But more lives have been lost off the San Francisco headlands. First came the 1,106-ton coastal steamer* City of Chester, *cut in half by the incoming inter-continental passenger liner* Oceanic *on a foggy morning in August 1888. Despite valiant attempts by the* Oceanic's *Chinese crew to save passengers from the other ship — some even leapt into the water to help — 16 passengers drowned that day.*

In 1901, the City of Rio de Janeiro *set the record for the worst maritime disaster in local history. At 4 a.m. on February 22, 1901, the steamship, piloted by master mariner Frederick Jordon, raised anchor and proceeded in the dark toward the Golden Gate. U.S. Consul General Rounceville Wildman was on board, and needed to catch the morning train. Fog closed in, but the pilot continued, only to hit the rocks. Within three minutes, the lights below deck failed, trapping those below. As the ship filled with water, 128 of the 210 people on board went to a watery grave.*

Ocean house, & Entrance to harbour from the Pacific. San Fransisco.

The 543-ton bark Brignardello *had only made two trips to Italy and back before losing her way in the mornings mists in September 1868 and grounding on Ocean Beach. The crew managed to unload a thousand cases of nuts before the owner gave up and sold the bark, and all her cargo, to a man named Meyer for $8,050. Before Meyer resold her—still wrecked on the beach—he managed to salvage a profitable portion of the marble, olive oil, chicory and vermouth in her hold. Two more owners attempted salvage before she was broken up by dynamite and winter waves in early 1869.*

$\int$

Clifftops & Back Corners

A S W I N D S A N D W A V E S G R I N D away at the hundred-year-old foundations of Sutro's once glorious baths, sand fills the cracks and crannies,
feathery grasses obscure the straight edges, and bright green algae
carpets the seawall.

A hundred years have passed since Sutro built his recreational
wonderland by the sea, and without his grand vision and fat wallet to
sustain them San Francisco's headlands offer only a shadow of their
Victorian attractions. But Lands End's most central attraction — the
oceanfront — remains ever present, and its wilder clifftops and back
corners host diverse flora, fauna and other wonders.

Wildlife and Wetlands

Lands End isn't an easy place for wildlife to live, what with the
City next door, the exposure to the ocean, and constant changes in
their environment. Despite these drawbacks, quail, swallows, wrens,
robins and waxwings frequent the woodlands; ravens and gulls nest in
the seacliffs; sea lions haul out on secluded beaches and offshore
rocks; squirrels burrow in the sand; and the occasional peregrine fal-
con perches on a clifftop snag where the air currents and easily visible
prey make good hunting grounds. Biologists estimate that as many
as 140 species of birds, 41 mammals, and 14 amphibians and reptiles
occur in the area.

The geography of the headlands, and their crown of forests,
helps winged creatures migrate easily from Marin to San Francisco and
back again. Migrating nuthatches, grosbeaks, warblers and other song-
birds, as well as butterflies, use the Lands End forests to build up
energy reserves before making the taxing crossing of the Golden Gate
channel or to rest up after a crossing.

Meanwhile, the ruined bath house provides an added bonus
for wildlife. The basin Sutro carved out of the cove to trap waves is
now a permanent pool of brackish water — half salt from the ocean and
half fresh from the spring that once supplied Sutro's icy plunge tank.
Gulls alight here to clean the salt off their wings and tufted ducks —

Picnic in the Gun Battery
*Dug into the highest
bluffs over Point Lobos
are the three coast
artillery batteries of Fort
Miley, built at the turn of
the century. Battery
Chester's rifles could fire
a 1,100-pound projectile
at an enemy ship, while
Batteries Springer and
Livingston lobbed shells
from their 12-inch mor-
tars onto its decks. The
National Park Service
recently converted these
battery grounds into pic-
nic sites offering lawns,
tables and stunning
views down the coast.*

rare Siberian visitors with jaunty head tassels — have been known to stop by for a protected paddle.

Other wetlands ring the basin where freshwater seeps moisten the soil. Both the pool and the surrounding wetlands sustain 24 water-tolerant plant species including curly-topped umbrella sedge and orange-blossomed nasturtium. The seeps also provide essential fresh water to local birds and mammals.

Endangered Birds & Beetles

For several species, Lands End may offer a rare scrap of habitat in an urban peninsula — habitat so rare that their future as a species is in danger. The California redlegged frog, for example, lives in fresh-water pools, streams and wetlands — most of which have been culverted, channelized or filled in throughout the Bay Area for urban flood control. In the scattered seeps of Lands End, however, a few of these 5-inch-long leggy amphibians have found a home. Ironically, this habitat lies within jumping distance of one of the original sources of the frog's demise. Its legs, sauteed in butter and white wine, frequently appeared on the Cliff House menu.

In the dunes below the Cliff House lives the bumblebee scarab beetle — another candidate for government listing as a threatened, rare or endangered species. The back of this tiny golden brown insect is so hairy it looks like a bumblebee or miniature bear. When famed geneticist J.S. Haldane was asked whether his biology studies suggested anything about God, he replied: "Only that he had an inordinant fondness

Birds on the Rocks
Flocks of shorebirds inhabit the surf-swept zone between land and sea, and among these, black oystercatchers choose some of the coast's most exposed spots. Pairs of these all-black, compact birds have built shell and pebble-lined nests on Seal Rocks, a roost dominated by gulls and cormorants. The oystercatchers search the marine terraces and ledges exposed by low tide for mussels, barnacles and other bivalves, prying open their shells using their long, red, chisel-shaped beaks.

for beetles." Although beetle species come in the hundreds of thousands (by comparison, all species of vertebrate animals total fewer than 44,000), the bumblebee is a rare one. Pedestrian trampling, European dune grass (the beetle prefers munching on native grasses) and development continue to encroach on its limited central California coast habitat.

Invasion of the Exotics

Lands End is so close to San Francisco's back gardens and the arboretum of coastal plants from all over the world at Sutro Heights, that many exotic species now vie with natives for the scarce soils of the continent's edge. Hardy natives such as the tall yellow bush lupine, which Spanish explorers noted seeing here in the 1700s, remain abundant but other species less so. Here and there on an outcrop of serpentine or chert, the rare coast rock cress is the first to bloom each spring — brightening Lands End with points of pink and purple.

On the old dune slopes grow the equally rare dune tansy and yarrow, both of which enjoy legendary medicinal value. The tansy, a yellow aromatic daisy-like plant, survives well in moving sand conditions. Its feathery leaves sport soft gray hairs which help the tansy absorb and diffuse the hot sun.

To encourage native plants to flourish in the area, the National Park Service has been replanting native California dune grass on fledgling dunes, and brightening the landscape elsewhere with native poppies, lupines, and coyote brush.

Deadly Coastline

Not so long ago, a big wave snuck up on a little girl exploring the Sutro Baths seawall. The wave knocked her into the ocean, where icy waters and strong currents sucked her under in seconds. She never surfaced again. Back on August 29, 1946, two schoolboys got stuck when a small landslide wiped out the trail up the cliff, and the incoming high tide flooded the beach and licked at their feet. Firemen formed a human chain to save them, but many others aren't so lucky. Tragic events plague Lands End, where 6 to 8 visitors get in trouble on the cliffs every year, and where over a dozen people have lost their lives in the past decade.

Walks on the Wild Side

City dwellers in search of coastal drama will find it on Lands End, now part of the world's largest urban national park. The area's main trail follows the clifftop route of the old Ferries and Cliff House Railroad, winding its way around Point Lobos, skirting seastacks and rusting shipwrecks, traversing the actual promontory known as Lands End, venturing across landslides, and meandering on past Painted Rock, Deadman's Point and Eagle Point to the Palace of the Legion of Honor.

The trail immerses visitors in oceanfront theatrics — bewitching eyes with Golden Gate views, filling ears with roaring surf and blasting fog horns, challenging feet with soft sand and crumbly rock, prickling skin with frosty breezes, damp mists and intermittent sun.

ON A GRAY, WINDY DAY, of which there are many, Lands End seems tantalizingly sinister with its precipitous steeps, unceasing onslaught of wind and waves, and mysterious black forests. But perhaps it is just this sense of precariousness, of venturing out onto the edge of the world, that has thrilled visitors to San Francisco's Pacific shore for over a century.

500 A.D. Earliest known Native American use of Lands End area.

1776 Spanish settlement of San Francisco peninsula.

1848 Rancho Punta de Lobos, a large Mexican land grant including San Francisco Headlands, becomes U.S. territory.

1850s First homestead established at Point Lobos by a potato farmer named Chambers.

Ocean House and Seal Rock House offer early seaside saloons.

1863 Real estate tycoon Charles Butler and partners build Point Lobos Toll Road from city to coast.

First Cliff House erected and opened by Butler.

1868 Butler enlarges Cliff House to three times its original size.

1881 Engineer Adolph Sutro purchases a cottage and surrounding lands above Cliff House.

1883 Butler sells Cliff House to Sutro.

1885 Sutro opens the gates to Sutro Heights – a formal garden around his cottage – to the local populace.

1887 *Parallel* shipwrecks and explodes on Cliff House rocks, damaging the building.

Congress declares Seal Rocks a marine sanctuary.

1888 Ferries and Cliff House Railroad offer first affordable public transit to San Francisco's Outside Lands.

1894 Sutro puts finishing touches on the three-acre glass palace of Sutro Baths after a seven-year construction period.

Fire burns first Cliff House to the ground.

1896 Sutro hosts gala opening of the second Cliff House, a Victorian gingerbread palace.

1898 Sutro dies.

1907 Second Cliff House burns.

1908 Sutro's daughter commences work on third and latest Cliff House, and completes it a year later.

1950s Whitney brothers enlarge Cliff House and modernize exterior to its present configuration.

1966 Sutro Baths goes up in flames.

1970s Cliff House, Sutro Heights and Sutro Baths become part of Golden Gate National Recreation Area.

ABOUT THE CLIFF HOUSE AND LANDS END

What to see:
The Cliff House Visitor Center, open from 10 a.m. to 4:30 p.m. daily, presents exhibits on local history and offers numerous books, cards and posters featuring the park and its environs.

Walks around Sutro Heights and the Sutro Baths ruins give the best hints of Sutro's heyday.

Get a bite and warm up after a Lands End walk where the old-timers did. The Cliff House is open for food and beverages every day of the week.

The Lands End Trail offers a long walk or jog between the Cliff House area and the Palace of the Legion of Honor.

When to visit:
The best times to visit are spring (when the wildflowers are in bloom) and fall (when the weather's warm and relatively fog-free).

What to look out for:
The terrain is extremely unstable and dangerous. Stay on trails to ensure your own safety.

At the water's edge, watch out for sneaker waves and keep an eye on tides (which can come in quickly and cut off your return route).

What to wear:
Bring a sweater and a windbreaker. Lands End bears the full brunt of Pacific winds and temperatures, and is often the last place the fog burns off.

Suggested Reading

Blaisdell, Marilyn. SAN FRANCISCANA PHOTOGRAPHS OF THE CLIFF HOUSE. San Francisco: Marilyn Blaisdell, 1985.

Blaisdell, Marilyn. SAN FRANCISCANA PHOTOGRAPHS OF THE SUTRO BATHS. San Francisco: Marilyn Blaisdell, 1985.

Delgado, James and Haller, Stephen. SHIPWRECKS AT THE GOLDEN GATE. San Francisco: Lexikos, 1989.

Gilliam, Harold. THE NATURAL WORLD OF SAN FRANCISCO. Garden City: Doubleday, 1967.

Jackson, Donald Dale. "Sutro Baths: The Greatest Show on Water." SMITHSONIAN, February 1993, 23:11, pp.120-132.

Stewart, Robert E., and Mary Frances. ADOLPH SUTRO, A BIOGRAPHY. Berkeley: Howell-North, 1962.

About the Author

Ariel Rubissow has been writing on Bay Area environmental and recreational topics for over 10 years. Her stories have appeared in the *San Francisco Chronicle and Examiner* and in the publications of the Sierra Club, the Trust for Public Land, the San Francisco Estuary Project and other organizations. She's also the author of *Golden Gate National Recreation Area Park Guide*.

The Golden Gate National Park Association wishes to thank the staff of the Golden Gate National Recreation Area who helped review and produce this publication.

GGNPA Production Management
Charles Money
Greg Moore

Editor
Nora L. Deans

Design
Nancy E. Koc

Photography
All photographs and hand tinting by Thea Schrack except:

GGNRA Archives (pages 17-top, 20, 28)
National Maritime Museum Library (pages 14-15, 17-bottom, 26, 27, 31, 32-middle, 33, 36, 37)
Jim Milestone (page 8)
Brenda Tharp (pages 7, 41, back cover)

Illustrations
Marilyn Blaisdell Collection (pages 18, 24-25)
California Academy of Sciences (pages 2, 10, 22, 29, 30, 32-top, 46)
Ann Caudle, © 1993 Monterey Bay Aquarium (pages 9, 40-top)
Pieter Folkens (page 21)
Karen Montgomery (page 4)
Lawrence Ormsby (pages 3, 13, 39, 40-bottom, 41)

Calligraphy
Lilly Lee (page 26)

Set in Sabon Antiqua

Printed in Hong Kong on recycled paper